HER MAJESTY
QUEEN
ELIZABETH
II

Platinum Jubilee Celebration
70 Years: 1952–2022

HER MAJESTY
QUEEN
ELIZABETH
II

Platinum Jubilee Celebration
70 Years: 1952–2022

Brian Hoey

Contents

The Woman Who is The Queen 6

Early Days 16

The Accession 24

The Coronation 28

The First Decade: 1952–1961 32

The Second Decade: 1962–1971 40

The Queen's Working Day 46

The Third Decade: 1972–1981 58

The Fourth Decade: 1982–1991 64

The Fifth Decade: 1992–2001 70

The Sixth Decade: 2002–2011 76

The Seventh Decade: 2012–2021 80

The Future 88

Acknowledgements 96

LEFT: Baby Princess Elizabeth with her parents: her mother the Duchess of York, who was Lady Elizabeth Bowes-Lyon before her marriage, and her father the Duke of York, who would later become George VI.

OPPOSITE: Her Majesty The Queen in France in 2014, attending a State Banquet hosted by President François Hollande, part of the ceremonies marking the 70th anniversary of D-Day.

The Woman Who is The Queen

Elizabeth II is the most famous woman in the world and yet, arguably, she is also one of the most private. When she was born on 21 April 1926 at 17 Bruton Street in London's Mayfair, the family home of her maternal grandparents, the Earl and Countess of Strathmore, it was the only time a future Queen would be born in a private house, not a palace or a castle. And for those who like to know such things, the year of her birth also saw the appearance for the first time on London's streets of red telephone boxes, which later became ubiquitous.

The Queen's public image is recognised in every country on earth, but very few people know the person behind the regal smile, the courtly wave. We have all seen her in a variety of guises: on countless stamps, coins and banknotes; dressed in her formal robes at the State Opening of Parliament, the only time, apart from her Coronation, when she wears a crown; in the colourful cloak and bonnet of the

Order of the Garter as she processes to St George's Chapel, Windsor, each June for the annual service of the Order; until 1986 in the scarlet uniform of the particular Guards regiment whose Colour was being Trooped, when she took the salute at the Trooping the Colour Parade. Since 1987 she has appeared at the ceremony in ordinary day clothes (but wearing the regimental badge) and travels by carriage, as she no longer rides on horseback at the head of her troops. Some of us have been fortunate enough to see her at closer quarters in her own home when she acts as hostess to several thousand guests during one of the summer Garden Parties. Each image is different and each of us has a view about the woman who has been our Queen since 1952.

It is to Her Majesty that the nation turns in moments of great celebration such as in her Diamond Jubilee Year, 2012, when hundreds of thousands of her subjects collected outside Buckingham Palace in the pouring rain, calling for her to appear, and also in times of national mourning, such as at the funeral of Diana, Princess of Wales in 1997.

The Queen has a natural dignity and, of course, perfect manners. One of her longest-serving courtiers said the reason why Her Majesty might sometimes come across as cold is that she has the very English reserve that appears to border on indifference, and to some outsiders this is seen as arrogance, a characteristic she certainly does not possess. She is completely without prejudice, treating everyone the same, no matter where they come from or their station in life. She is as likely to stop and chat with one of her stable-lads as with the Archbishop of Canterbury – probably more likely as they would have more in common. She bestows her friendship cautiously, but once given it is there for life and she regards loyalty as by far the most important of personal qualities.

Her Majesty has performed her role as sovereign with flawless professionalism since the day she acceded to the throne aged just 25. During that time she has served longer than any Pope (seven) – Pius XII, John XXIII, Paul VI, John Paul I, John Paul II, Benedict XVI, Francis; any Archbishop of Canterbury (seven) – Geoffrey Fisher, Michael Ramsey, Donald Coggan, Robert Runcie, George Carey, Rowan Williams, Justin Welby; any US President (14) – Harry S. Truman, Dwight D. Eisenhower, John F. Kennedy, Lyndon B. Johnson, Richard Nixon, Gerald Ford, Jimmy Carter, Ronald Reagan, George H.W. Bush, Bill Clinton, George W. Bush, Barack Obama, Donald Trump, Joe Biden; or any British Prime

Dressed in the blue velvet mantles and plumed velvet hats of the Knights of the Garter, The Queen, Prince Charles and Prince William process on Garter Day at Windsor Castle in 2013. As Sovereign of the Order of the Garter, pinned to her mantle Her Majesty wears the Garter Star which was a gift from her father, King George VI, when she was invested into the Noble Order of the Garter.

Minister (14, or 15 if you count Harold Wilson's two terms). They are Winston Churchill, Antony Eden, Harold Macmillan, Alec Douglas-Home, Harold Wilson (1), Edward Heath, Harold Wilson (2), James Callaghan, Margaret Thatcher (her first female Prime Minister), John Major, Tony Blair, Gordon Brown, David Cameron, Theresa May and Boris Johnson, with Blair, Cameron, May and Johnson not even born when she came to the throne.

The Queen's first Prime Minister, Sir Winston Churchill, invited himself to Balmoral during the first year of her reign. At 78 he was by far the oldest guest; the Queen was only 26 at the time but he reminded Her Majesty that he had also been a guest there of King Edward VII, Her Majesty's great-grandfather, with whom he shared similar tastes in fine cigars and very large brandies.

Queen Elizabeth II and Britain's Prime Minister Winston Churchill, along with Prime Ministers and senior ministers from other Commonwealth countries, at the Commonwealth Economic Conference held at Buckingham Palace in December 1952.

Elizabeth II is without doubt an accomplished stateswoman whose store of knowledge is unrivalled. She became Head of the Commonwealth by acclamation, not by right simply because she was Queen, and every single member of that eclectic group admits that she is the cement that holds the organisation together.

At the age of 25, Elizabeth Alexandra Mary, the first child of King George VI and his Consort, Queen Elizabeth, became the 42nd sovereign of England since William the Conqueror, yet only its sixth Queen Regnant. She is now the longest-reigning British monarch since Queen Victoria, who was the last Queen Regnant and reigned for 63 years, while their joint ancestor, Elizabeth I, reigned for 44 years.

Elizabeth II is also the first female sovereign to bear the family name of Windsor that was adopted by her grandfather, King George V, in 1917 during the First World War, to avoid accusations that the monarchy was German.

As heir presumptive, the young Princess Elizabeth received special tuition in law and constitutional history to prepare her for her future role as sovereign. When she succeeded her father, King George VI, on 6 February 1952, Elizabeth had been married for five years and had two small children – Prince Charles, born in 1948, and Princess Anne, born in 1950. The Queen and her husband, the Duke of Edinburgh, had hoped for a few more years, at least, in which to enjoy a relatively normal family life; but it was not to be. The responsibilities of monarchy have taken precedence over all else, and public duties – which she has never been tempted to avoid – invariably have first call on The Queen's time and energy.

As a constitutional monarch, Her Majesty's powers are awesome – but only in theory. She controls all the Armed Forces, so she could sell all the ships in the Royal Navy, the tanks in the Army and every aircraft used by the Royal Air Force. Wars are declared in her name, ambassadors from foreign countries are accredited to her Court of St James's and nothing in Britain becomes law until her Royal Assent has been granted. Of course, all this is just window dressing. She cannot do any of these things on her own. In practice, these decisions are taken by the elected government of the day. So the saying 'she reigns but does not rule' is a literal truth.

King George V and Queen Mary visiting a shipyard in Birkenhead in 1917, the year that the Royal Family's name changed from the House of Saxe-Coburg-Gotha to the House of Windsor.

The Queen was crowned in Westminster Abbey on 2 June 1953 when her full titles were revealed as: Elizabeth the Second, by the Grace of God, of the United Kingdom of Great Britain and Northern Ireland and of her other Realms and Territories Queen, Head of the Commonwealth, Defender of the Faith. She was not, and never was to become, Empress, as India, from which the title was taken, had been granted independence in 1947, the year she was married.

In the 70 years she has been on the throne, The Queen has never put a foot wrong in her public or private life. An affectionate wife, loving mother (with two more children, Andrew and Edward, being born while she was Queen), a devoted grandmother and great-grandmother – these characteristics have never impinged on her devotion to duty. This is the quality she possesses above all others. In many ways she has sacrificed a normal family life to the demands of public office.

Princess Elizabeth, in her role as Colonel-in-Chief, inspects soldiers of the 16th/5th Lancers at Lulworth Camp in Dorset, 1948.

The Queen and Prince Philip following the Royal Maundy service at Leicester Cathedral in April 2017. Prince Philip retired from public duty in August that year, so it was the last time he attended the Maundy Thursday event.

The Queen has served her country with dignity and devotion and has borne the marital problems of her late sister and three of her children with fortitude. She has also been forced to accept the deep sadness of the loss of her sister, mother and, of course, her beloved husband, Prince Philip, who died just weeks before his 100th birthday. A very private woman by inclination, she has been forced to live most of her life in the full glare of public attention. It is not a position she has found to her liking, but one she has accepted with grace and dignity, or, as Prince Philip used to say, 'It goes with the job.'

Her Majesty's reign has been the most informal of Britain's 1,000-year monarchy and she has made herself more accessible than any of her distinguished predecessors through her television and radio broadcasts. Because of her personal qualities, royal remoteness has all but disappeared, and she, together with other members of the Royal Family, now displays a working side where once only ceremonial and privilege were seen. But nobody who meets her is ever left in any doubt about who and what she is. She is fully aware of her position and nobody is foolish enough to confuse her friendliness with an invitation for them to attempt to become overly familiar.

The Queen has always had a soft spot for the Armed Forces, dating back to the days of the Second World War, when she pleaded with her father to be allowed to join one of the services, in any capacity. And on VE (Victory in Europe) Day in 1945, she and Margaret were sneaked out of Buckingham Palace with a small group

The Queen has always loved dogs; here at Royal Lodge, Windsor in 1937, the young Princess Elizabeth and her sister Princess Margaret enjoy spending time with the family pets.

of young officers and mingled with the crowds shouting for the King. It was the last time she would ever experience being just 'one of the people'.

At heart she is still a country woman enjoying few things more than being alone on horseback, even in her 90s (without a protective hard hat), or walking with her dogs. She still drives a car – without wearing a seat belt – and she has recently, albeit reluctantly, adapted to the modern world of computer technology, using an encrypted mobile phone, iPad and Skype. But the communications equipment on her desk in Buckingham Palace still looks like something from the 1940s and 50s – which it probably is. And when her private secretary brings the post to her sitting room every morning, he still carries it in a small wicker basket. Her Majesty is one of the wealthiest women on earth but her personal habits border on the frugal, though there is no truth in the rumour that she haunts the corridors of Buckingham Palace late at night switching off the lights.

The future of the House of Windsor has been assured with the births of a son, Prince Charles, grandson, Prince William, and great-grandson, Prince George, but many people believe that for the continued stability of the monarchy in Britain, it is to be hoped that Elizabeth II has inherited the longevity genes of her own mother, Queen Elizabeth the Queen Mother, who lived to be 101. The Queen is generally in excellent health and if that continues then we have more years in which to enjoy an Elizabethan reign of unparalleled responsibility and utter dedication. She exemplifies all that is best in a constitutional monarch, and has clearly demonstrated that nothing is allowed to interfere with the office of sovereign and the role that is a job for life.

In 1991, President Ronald Reagan succinctly summed up the attitude and feelings of many people when he said, 'Throughout the world, with all due respect to every other female monarch, whenever we speak about "The Queen" we all know which one we are referring to.' He was right. Elizabeth II is unique; the acceptable face of what to some is an outmoded institution, and even those who disagree with everything she stands for admit, perhaps grudgingly, that she has earned widespread respect and admiration as one of the most remarkable individuals in the world.

Her Majesty has a natural dignity that one would expect from the sovereign, but also an innate graciousness that is a very special trait. When meeting people from any walk of life, she has the ability to make you feel you are the one person she has always wanted to talk to. She never looks over your shoulder to see if there is someone more important in the room. And what some people mistake for shyness is, in fact, complete self-confidence. There is not a single ounce of self-doubt in The Queen's make-up.

More than any of her predecessors, The Queen has introduced a personal style to the monarchy, travelling to over a hundred countries during her reign and meeting more people than all of her ancestors put together. To watch Her Majesty with other world leaders is to witness a masterclass in diplomacy. She is far and away the most experienced stateswoman in the world – and it shows. When she spoke to former President George W. Bush, then the most powerful man on earth, she was able to remind him of some of the subjects she discussed with his father ten years earlier when he was President of the United States.

Elizabeth II is a remarkable woman – or as she once put it, 'An ordinary woman who has found herself in an extraordinary position.' She is, quite simply, the perfect example of a constitutional monarch. She is unique, in her mid 90s, to still be a working sovereign and clearly a woman who continues to fulfil her destiny. She is The Queen.

Early Days

Although Princess Elizabeth was the first, and only, future sovereign to be born in a private house, she still entered a world surrounded by privilege and luxury. Her parents were the Duke and Duchess of York, as her father was the second son of the monarch, King George V.

At the time of her birth the infant Princess was third in the line of succession to the throne, after her Uncle David, the Prince of Wales, and, of course, her own father. But as the Prince of Wales was only 31 and fully expected to one day marry and produce an heir, Elizabeth was not expected to be a future monarch.

In later life, The Queen said that she enjoyed an idyllic childhood, surrounded by love and laughter. Her parents undertook a number of public duties but they spent part of every day with their young daughter and four years later, when Princess Margaret was born, with them both. What was unusual in families of their rank and

status was that every morning the children would run into their parents' bedroom and have what they called 'high jinks'. And, indeed, Princess Elizabeth still popped in to see her mother and father every morning right up to the day she was married in 1947.

Like many tiny children, Elizabeth found it difficult to say some names correctly. Her first nanny was Mrs Clara Knight, but as Elizabeth could not pronounce Clara, she made it Allah, and that's what she remained. Elizabeth was also a problem name, so that became Lilibet, a soubriquet that has stayed with her throughout her life – but only to her immediate family. When Princess Margaret Rose was born, Elizabeth called her 'Bud' – 'as she is not a full grown rose yet'.

Education was not considered to be of high priority for Elizabeth, whose grandfather, King George V, had refused permission for her to go to boarding school, saying that all he wanted was for her to be taught good handwriting. Nobody was interested in trying to make the Princess an academic or intellectual, so there was no emphasis on study, apart from French, which she learned from an early age.

The family home was 145 Piccadilly, overlooking the gardens of Buckingham Palace, where they lived for nine and a half years. A Scottish governess, Miss Marion Crawford, was engaged and soon became known as Crawfie. She believed it was important that Elizabeth – and her young sister, Margaret – should see something of the outside world. Elizabeth in particular loved to look out of the window at the people passing by in Piccadilly and also at the famous London red buses. She often asked Crawfie where all the people were going, so Crawfie took the children on a short bus ride one day, with Elizabeth demanding that they ride upstairs. Crawfie also handed Elizabeth some pennies so she could pay for her own fare. On another occasion they travelled on the Underground, which Elizabeth described as 'exciting'. Of course, these events happened in the days when only the King was accompanied by a personal police protection officer, so Crawfie and the royal children went about London entirely on their own, with no problems.

The first major tragedy in Elizabeth's life occurred at exactly five minutes to midnight on 20 January 1936. That was the moment when her beloved grandfather, King George V, died and her Uncle David became His Majesty King Edward VIII. When Elizabeth was told the news of her grandfather's death she was devastated and broke down in tears. Her grandmother, Queen Mary, who had maintained a stiff upper lip and never showed any emotion, gently told Elizabeth what had happened

Crawfie (front left) took her young royal charges, Princesses Elizabeth and Margaret, on a boat trip in 1940.

and then guided her through her grief, explaining that royals do not display feelings of sadness or extreme happiness in public. It was a lesson that the Princess quickly learned and one she has employed throughout her long life.

The reign of Edward VIII lasted for only 325 days before he abdicated in order to marry an American divorcee, Mrs Wallis Simpson, and move out of Britain for the rest of his life.

For Elizabeth it meant a complete change. Not only would she become first in the line of succession as her father ascended the throne, but she would also have to move across the road to Buckingham Palace, which the family did on 15 February 1937. At first Elizabeth was horrified at the move, but she grew to love the place and she and Margaret enjoyed playing in its long corridors.

During the first year of the new reign, the first big occasion Elizabeth attended was, of course, her father's Coronation at Westminster Abbey. It took place on 12 May 1937. Elizabeth and Margaret were dressed alike in pretty dresses with tiny coronets specially ordered by their father. Elizabeth also had a short train added to her dress, much to the annoyance of her little sister.

Hidden away in the Royal Library at Windsor Castle is a short document that has been treasured for over 80 years. Wrapped in pink ribbon, and handwritten by

the ten-year-old Princess Elizabeth, it is her personal account of what happened on that historic day. She decided to write an essay for 'Mummy and Papa in Memory of their Coronation as a gift from Lilibet By Herself'. She described the weather, which was dreadful, and how she looked out of her window at Buckingham Palace to see the crowds waiting outside, some of whom had been camped out all night. She captured the excitement of the day as only a child could. If the document ever came up for auction, which it won't, it would sell for hundreds of thousands of pounds.

When the Second World War broke out in 1939, the family was at Balmoral Castle. The King and Queen immediately returned to London, but moved Elizabeth and Margaret to the comparative safety of Windsor where they lived at Royal Lodge. At night they slept in the cellars at Windsor Castle and Princess Elizabeth said she found it very strange to see the sentries on guard dressed in khaki uniforms instead of their peacetime scarlet tunics and bearskins. But even at Windsor it was a cloistered life with little contact with the outside world. It was also at Windsor that the Princess first received serious riding tuition and her instructor was pleasantly surprised when his young charge wanted to know how much it cost to feed a horse.

Elizabeth was also taught history by the Vice-Provost of nearby Eton College, who made no distinction between his royal pupil and anyone else, often marking her essays with 'N' for Nonsense.

Towards the end of the war, shortly before her 19th birthday, Princess Elizabeth joined the Army as a Second Subaltern in the ATS (Auxiliary Territorial Service) with the serial number she still remembers: 230873. Her father was against it, saying it would undermine her future position. He finally agreed only on condition that she did not sleep in camp alongside her fellow officers; his daughter had to return to Windsor instead, much to her annoyance. But the experience of being among young women of similar age, from different backgrounds, gave her the opportunity of testing herself against them and she acquitted herself well. She learned to drive and service heavy vehicles, and how to handle a rifle, even if her military service lasted for only six weeks.

As the war ended, the nation went wild for a time. After six years of hardship, and even though rationing of everything from food to clothes to petrol would

Coronation Day 1937: standing alongside her mother Queen Elizabeth, father King George VI and sister Princess Margaret, an excited Princess Elizabeth performs a perfect example of a royal wave from the balcony at Buckingham Palace.

Confident in the saddle from a young age, Princess Elizabeth rides out in Windsor Great Park with her uncle, Prince Henry, Duke of Gloucester, in 1936.

remain for several years, it meant that at last people could enjoy themselves without worrying about bombs falling.

Unlike most upper-class young women of her age, by this time Princess Elizabeth had never had a date with any man. She was not permitted to go out alone with anyone – suitable or not. In any event, since the age 13, there was only ever going to be one man for her: Prince Philip. The handsome young naval officer had survived the war and Elizabeth was determined that he would be the man in her life. The feeling was mutual and, in spite of the King's reluctance, they became secretly engaged towards the end of 1946. Finally, His Majesty agreed to their marriage, which took place on 20 November 1947.

There was still a shortage of clothes so the Prime Minister allowed the bride an extra 100 coupons so she could have the silk wedding dress she wanted. The wedding

On 10 July 1947, Buckingham Palace officially announced Princess Elizabeth's engagement to Lieutenant Philip Mountbatten, RN; her engagement ring used diamonds from a tiara belonging to Prince Philips's mother.

The wedding ceremony of Princess Elizabeth and the Duke of Edinburgh in progress at Westminster Abbey. Norman Hartnell designed the bride's wedding gown and here the embroidered silk tulle train is displayed to full effect by the pageboys, her cousins Prince William of Gloucester and Prince Michael of Kent.

was a grand spectacle, with the Household Cavalry donning pre-war full ceremonial dress uniform, complete with black bearskins and drawn swords. Inside Westminster Abbey were 2,500 guests, including no fewer than six kings and seven queens. Just before the wedding, Prince Philip had been created Duke of Edinburgh and Earl of Merioneth, but the titles were gazetted only on the wedding day itself. Back at Buckingham Palace, the wedding party of 150 guests (the others at the service had to make their own arrangements) sat down to a comparatively modest feast of Filet de Sole Mountbatten and Bombe Glacée Princesse Elizabeth.

As there was no possibility of a foreign honeymoon, the couple spent the first part of their life together at Broadlands, the Hampshire home of Lord Mountbatten. It was the start of a marriage that would last for 73 years, and would only end when Prince Philip died in April 2021.

LEFT: Princess Elizabeth and the Duke of Edinburgh are welcomed on their arrival at Nairobi airport in Kenya in February 1952 at the start of their Commonwealth tour; sadly, it was to be cut short just days later when news of the death of her father, King George VI, was received.

OPPOSITE: Having ascended the throne earlier that year, in November 1952 The Queen, with Prince Philip beside her, travels to her first State Opening of Parliament. Her Majesty has only missed the event twice during her reign: in 1959 and 1963 when she was expecting her two youngest children.

The Accession

'By the sudden death of my dear father I am called upon to assume the duties and responsibility of sovereignty.'

These were the words of Her Majesty Queen Elizabeth II in her simple yet moving Accession Speech on 8 February 1952, just 36 hours after she had learned that her father, King George VI, had died. At the age of 25, Elizabeth Alexandra Mary became the 42nd sovereign of England since William the Conqueror, yet only its sixth Queen Regnant.

She became Queen, without her immediate knowledge, in the early hours of 6 February 1952 while she was in Kenya at the start of a Commonwealth tour, en route to Australia and New Zealand. Her father had died in his sleep at Sandringham, having been at London Airport on 31 January to see her and the Duke of Edinburgh off on their proposed tour. His Majesty, a heavy smoker all his

adult life, had suffered ill health for many years – but the strain of becoming King after his brother's abdication and the difficulty of reigning during the Second World War had also taken their toll. He seemed to know that when he said farewell to his daughter at the airport, it was probably going to be for the last time and he would never see her again. She departed a Princess but would return a Queen.

Preparations had been made just in case they were needed, including the draft Accession Declaration, only to be used in the event of the King's death. Elizabeth was actually sitting on a high platform in the trees, part of the famous Treetops Hotel in the Aberdare Mountains, photographing the wildlife far below when her status changed. She and Philip were staying at Sagana Lodge, a wedding present from the people of Kenya, when Michael Parker, Prince Philip's aide, was told by telephone what had happened. Parker gave Philip the sad news; he received it like a 'bombshell had hit him'. The time in Kenya was 2.45pm when Philip gave his wife the world-changing news that her father had died and she was now Queen. It was the saddest news she could have received but immediately she adopted the regal composure that became an integral part of her life from then on. Her private secretary, Major Martin Charteris, who was staying nearby at the Outspan Hotel, later wrote that when he arrived to meet the new sovereign he found her 'very composed, the absolute master of her fate' and she was already at work drafting papers and letters of apology for the cancellation of the tour. He asked her by what regnal name she wished to be known. Her reply was simple and straightforward, 'My own name, of course – what else?' She could have chosen one of her other names – Alexandra or Mary – or even a different name from any former Queen.

The journey home from Africa involved several changes of aircraft as, of course, this was long before the days when jet travel meant transcontinental flight could be achieved in hours instead of days. The new Queen spent much of the time in the air discussing details about the Accession Council and the announcement that would be made from the balcony at St James's Palace. There was a ritual and protocol that had to be observed with the accession of a new sovereign, and her private secretary, who had been prepared for months for such an occasion, explained every little item, underlining the legendary attention to detail that had become the hallmark of the Royal Household. As with every royal journey overseas, before and since, every member of the Royal Family travels with a complete outfit of mourning clothes in their luggage, so when The Queen arrived at London Airport she was dressed

The coffin bearing George VI travelled from Sandringham to London's King Cross station before making its onward journey to Westminster Hall. The veiled figures of His Majesty's wife and daughters are at the front of the group, on the right.

in black. On this occasion the precaution had also been taken of including a Royal Standard in the luggage.

Elizabeth's Uncle Harry, the Duke of Gloucester, came on board to welcome her, accompanied by Lord and Lady Mountbatten. Waiting on the tarmac was a small group of dignitaries, headed by the Prime Minister, Winston Churchill, who was so overcome with emotion that he found it almost impossible to speak. However, The Queen did not allow any of them to kiss her hand in obeisance. That privilege was reserved for her grandmother, Queen Mary, who was waiting at Clarence House and insisted that she would be the first of the royal ladies to curtsey to the new monarch. As she dropped a graceful, deep curtsey to her granddaughter, it was a moving, elegant and formal recognition of Elizabeth's new position. Queen Mary was the only Queen in British history to see her own granddaughter become sovereign.

The Accession Council was held at St James's Palace, as tradition required, with The Queen reading her Declaration of Sovereignty to the Privy Council. Later that same day, The Queen and Prince Philip drove to Sandringham where the King's body lay. He was brought to London on 11 February, lying in state at Westminster Hall for three days; some 300,000 people filed past to pay their last respects. And at his funeral at St George's Chapel, in Windsor Castle, The Queen walked alone immediately behind his coffin, as was her right as the new sovereign.

The Coronation

The Coronation of Queen Elizabeth II took place, as the 900-year-old tradition demanded, at Westminster Abbey on 2 June 1953. The date was chosen partly so that it would not interfere with the running of The Derby the next day, thereby pleasing both Her Majesty and the Duke of Norfolk, also an avid racegoer, who was in overall charge of the arrangements for the ceremony.

It was to be the first crowning to be shown live on television, but even here there was difficulty between the traditionalists and the modernisers, the former wanting to preserve the mystique of royalty, and the modernisers, led by the Duke of Edinburgh, believing it was important that everyone should be able to see the entire proceedings. A compromise was reached whereby the recognition, crowning and the homage would be seen live on television, but the most sacred part of the service, the anointing, would not be shown.

Sadly, Queen Mary was not there to see her granddaughter crowned. She had died at her home, Marlborough House, on 24 March 1953 at the age of 85, having left instructions in her will that if she died before the Coronation, her death should not interfere with the proposed schedule.

The day of the Coronation dawned dreary and wet, but it did little to dampen the enthusiasm of the 30,000-strong crowd who had camped out all night on The Mall to see the procession leave Buckingham Palace. There were no fewer than 29 foreign monarchies and scores of world leaders represented, with kings, queens, princes, princesses, sheiks and maharajahs, including the statuesque Queen Salote of Tonga who was extremely popular with the crowds.

The four-year-old Prince Charles had been brought in via a side door to sit between his grandmother, the Queen Mother, and his aunt, Princess Margaret, and throughout the long ceremony he behaved impeccably. In the procession inside Westminster Abbey was another young boy who would become known throughout the world in later life. The coronet of the Lord High Chancellor was carried by his page, a very young Master Andrew Parker Bowles; many years later his ex-wife, Camilla, married Prince Charles.

After the crowning with the heavy St Edward's Crown, and the anointing with holy oil made to a formula devised by Charles I, the first person to pay obeisance was The Queen's husband, the Duke of Edinburgh; wearing his peer's robes, he knelt and pledged his fidelity. Later Her Majesty left Westminster Abbey wearing the lighter Imperial State Crown, which she jokingly called 'My going away hat'.

Prince Charles at the Coronation ceremony, flanked by his grandmother (the Queen Mother) and aunt (Princess Margaret).

The Queen Mother and Duke of Edinburgh engage with the young Prince Charles and Princess Anne as the Royal Family gathers on the balcony of Buckingham Palace after the Coronation ceremony.

The newly crowned Queen was driven back to Buckingham Palace in the Gold State Coach, first used by King George III, drawn by eight Windsor greys. The Queen Mother and Princess Margaret were there to greet her, and Prince Charles and Princess Anne were running around, glad to be part of all the excitement. Her Majesty, of course, still had more duties to perform. First she had to allow the official Coronation photographs to be taken by Cecil Beaton, while still wearing the crown that had been on her head for three hours. Then it was out on to the balcony to watch the RAF fly-past.

Throughout the United Kingdom there were street parties in every town and city, and the ceremony was seen as the biggest single boost to the television industry, when previously fewer than one in every ten thousand homes possessed a set. Millions had witnessed at first hand this ancient ceremony and wonderful example of royal pageantry. It truly was the start of the new Elizabethan Age.

HEAVY LIES THE CROWN...

Legend has it that in preparation for her Coronation, The Queen, in order to get used to the weight of St Edward's Crown with which she would be crowned, walked around with 2lb (1kg) bags of sugar strapped to her head. The solid 22-carat gold St Edward's Crown, adorned with 444 jewels, was made for Charles II in 1661. It stands some 12 inches (30cm) tall and weighs 4.9lbs (2.23kg).

LEFT: The Queen and the Duke of Edinburgh walk through the cheering crowds in Stratford in the Taranaki region of New Zealand's North Island in January 1954.

OPPOSITE: Her Majesty Queen Elizabeth II, photographed in 1957.

The First Decade: 1952–1961

The first years of the new Elizabethan reign saw The Queen visiting her people in Britain and throughout the Commonwealth. She travelled the length and breadth of the United Kingdom, while the tour of the Commonwealth lasted 174 days and took her across Africa, Australia, New Zealand, the Middle East and the Caribbean. In late December 1953, and early the following year, Her Majesty and the Duke of Edinburgh visited first New Zealand and then Australia, where they received a rapturous welcome, particularly as The Queen was the first reigning monarch to visit the Antipodes.

In 1954, on the vessel's first voyage, *Britannia* carried The Queen and the Duke of Edinburgh home from Libya. Prince Charles and Princess Anne joined their parents for the last leg of the return journey on this historic voyage. Some years later, while she was in Fiji on board the Royal Yacht, Her Majesty was photographed

BUILDING THE ROYAL YACHT *BRITANNIA*

The commissioning of a new royal yacht was of major importance. The original estimate for the building of the yacht was £1,615,000, including £290,000 profit for the ship builders. Eventually, the final price was £2,098,000 – possibly the bargain of the century considering the number of nautical miles she would sail in her sea-going lifetime and the amount of business she generated when British exporters were allowed to hold important meetings on board. The Queen took an enormous personal interest in the design of *Britannia*. In the sitting room she wanted the country-house look of an open fireplace. The Admiralty pointed out that, under centuries-old naval rules, any open coal fireplace required the presence of two seamen at all times: one carrying a bucket of water, the other a bucket of sand, in case of fire. So the idea of a real fireplace was dropped and replaced with one that used electric bars.

turning the tables on cameramen by filming her own version of the tour on her 8mm cine camera.

As The Queen came to grips with the business of being monarch, the Duke of Edinburgh was forced to find a role for himself. There is no official constitutional role for the husband of The Queen; he wasn't even given the title of Consort, so he set about improving the inner workings of Buckingham Palace. He went through the place like a whirlwind and became the first ever member of any Royal Family to enter the palace kitchens. He found there were two separate kitchens: the first to serve only royalty and the second for everyone else. So he soon ordered the removal of the first and everyone now eats from the same kitchen. Her Majesty didn't interfere with his plans even if, privately, she did not entirely approve. After all, she had grown up surrounded by pomp and pageantry, so why change it?

Another first for Her Majesty occurred when, accompanied by Prince Philip, she attended the farewell dinner party for her Prime Minister, the 80-year-old Sir Winston Churchill, on the eve of his resignation, in 1955. Not only did she break with tradition by being the first sovereign ever to enter No.10 Downing Street, but she also proposed the health of her very special host. This was a response to Churcill's own toast to Her Majesty, during which he was visibly moved as he praised the British monarchy.

On 15 May 1954, thousands of people lined the banks of the River Thames to cheer as Queen Elizabeth II, Prince Philip and their children, Charles and Anne, sailed home on the Royal Yacht *Britannia* at the end of the Commonwealth tour which had taken six months.

The Queen arrives at Downing Street in 1955 for dinner with Sir Winston and Lady Churchill on the eve of his resignation.

In January 1956, The Queen and the Duke of Edinburgh paid an official visit to Nigeria, where the most moving moment occurred when the royal party stopped at a leper colony at Oji River. To the delight of the colony, Her Majesty and His Royal Highness decided to financially adopt a leper child.

For the Royal Family, 1957 was an eventful year. In February, The Queen created her husband a Prince of the United Kingdom, 100 years after Queen Victoria bestowed the same honour on her Consort, Prince Albert. The eight-year-old Prince Charles was enrolled as a boarder at Cheam Preparatory School, becoming the first royal heir to be educated outside of a royal palace. The Queen received an ecstatic welcome on her first visit since the Coronation to the United States, where 3,000 journalists and photographers were accredited to cover the tour. Then, to complete a memorable year, Her Majesty's Christmas broadcast was seen on television for the first time.

If ever there was a single incident that divided the nation on the monarchy and The Queen, it was the one that occurred in August 1957. A writer, historian and

politician named John Grigg, who had inherited the title of 2nd Baron Altrincham in 1955 – but who disclaimed his title in 1963 – made what appeared to be an unwarranted and vicious attack on Her Majesty. Writing in the *National and English Review* he said that the Court of Elizabeth II was 'too upper-class and British' and he advocated a more classless and Commonwealth Court; he also criticised The Queen's style of public speaking. Most of the British press attacked Grigg's article, but there was also a fair amount of support for his views. The Establishment turned its back on the author, with the BBC refusing him any airtime to explain his views. However, the independent Granada Television agreed to interview him. Grigg's article received worldwide publicity and did eventually achieve what he had set out to do. Among the first changes were debutantes no longer being presented at Court after 1958, and the Queen had some elocution lessons before she made her Christmas broadcast in 1957.

February 1960 was a significant month for the Royal Family, and for The Queen in particular. On 8 February it was announced from Buckingham Palace that Queen Elizabeth II had changed the family's surname. She declared it her 'will and pleasure' that in future her descendants should be called Mountbatten-Windsor, though she and her children would continue to be the House of Windsor. Then, on 19 February, Her Majesty gave birth to her second son, Prince Andrew, who was

OPPOSITE: The Queen in the Long Library at Sandringham, having just broadcast her first televised Christmas message, Christmas Day 1957.

RIGHT: Photographed at Balmoral in 1960, Princess Anne looks on as The Queen holds baby Prince Andrew.

almost ten years younger than his sister, Princess Anne, and over 11 years younger than his brother, Prince Charles.

In May 1960 came another happy event when The Queen's only sister, Princess Margaret, married the society photographer Antony Armstrong-Jones; he was later created Earl of Snowdon. Their honeymoon was spent on board the Royal Yacht *Britannia*, in the Caribbean. But Her Majesty was saddened later that year when South Africa decided to abolish the monarchy in their country. The Queen had long held South Africa in great affection; it was there that she had celebrated her 21st birthday, and she had worked strenuously to maintain the Commonwealth as a strong family unit. It was to be 33 years before South Africa would rejoin this unique organisation.

At the beginning of 1961, The Queen embarked on her first visit to India, with a five-week tour of the subcontinent that included Pakistan and Nepal, as well as stops in Cyprus, Iran and Italy. In Delhi, half a million people turned out to give her and the Duke an ecstatic welcome.

As the first decade of The Queen's reign drew to a close, it was clear that she had fulfilled her role faultlessly. Her Majesty remained as popular as ever and was admired wherever she went, at home and abroad. More than 25 million people – over half the population of the United Kingdom – either watched on television or listened on the radio to her Christmas broadcast in 1961.

The Queen's attention to matters of State had never faltered and her grasp of complex political affairs impressed even seasoned ministers with many more years' experience.

Princess Margaret's wedding to Antony Armstrong-Jones took place at Westminster Abbey on 6 May 1960; here the bride curtsies to her sister, The Queen, as the ceremony draws to a close.

The Queen waves to the crowds as she rides on an elephant in Benares during the royal tour of India in 1961; the Duke of Edinburgh rides on the elephant alongside her.

THE 1950S

After the privations of the Second World War, Britain was emerging to a new beginning and one of the first highlights of the decade was the ending of petrol rationing in 1950 after ten years. In 1952, what was to become the longest-running play in the world, Agatha Christie's *The Mousetrap*, opened at The Ambassadors Theatre in London, after a pre-West End tour, with Richard Attenborough and Sheila Sim in the leading roles. Just before the Coronation, on 29 May 1953 the New Zealand mountaineer Edmund Hillary, accompanied by Sherpa Tenzing, became the first person to reach the summit of Mount Everest, the highest mountain in the world. In 1957, Elvis Presley saw his record 'All Shook Up' reach No.1 in the UK charts.

The Second Decade: 1962–1971

In March 1963, The Queen was in Australia to help celebrate the Jubilee of the country's capital city, Canberra. To mark the occasion, she created the Prime Minister, Sir Robert Menzies, a Knight of the Order of the Thistle.

Back in Britain, Her Majesty was about to see the fourth Prime Minister of her reign. Harold Macmillan had announced that he was to leave office through ill health, and that his successor was to be the Earl of Home. Her Majesty was constitutionally bound to accept her Prime Minister's advice on such matters, and she therefore invited Lord Home to accept the post, which he did, renouncing his peerage a few days later and becoming known as Sir Alec Douglas-Home.

The Queen's uncle, the Duke of Windsor, was greatly cheered to receive a telegram from his favourite niece on his 70th birthday in 1964. He saw this as evidence of her desire to heal the bitterness within the Royal Family caused by

his abdication. Three years later, on 7 June 1967, came further moves towards reconciliation when The Queen invited the Duke and Duchess to attend the unveiling of a memorial plaque to Queen Mary at Marlborough House.

On 10 March 1964, The Queen gave birth to her fourth child, Prince Edward, at Buckingham Palace. He made his first public appearance in June of that year when The Queen carried him on to the balcony of the palace after the Sovereign's Birthday Parade, Trooping the Colour.

Two important overseas visits took place in 1965: the first, in February, was to Ethiopia, where Emperor Haile Selassie declared that the welcome given to Her Majesty was the greatest ever extended to a visiting Head of State, with over 200,000 men, women and children lining the route from the airport to the royal palace alone. The second visit was in May, when The Queen became the first British monarch in 56 years to visit Germany. The most dramatic moment of the ten-city tour was when Her Majesty came face to face with the stark symbol of a divided Europe – the Berlin Wall.

LEFT: The Queen and the Duke of Edinburgh visiting the Berlin Wall on their State Visit to Germany in 1965.

OPPOSITE: Actor Peter O'Toole is presented to The Queen at the Odeon Theatre in London's Leicester Square following the world premiere of the film *Lawrence of Arabia* in 1962, in which O'Toole took the title role.

The Commonwealth has always held a special place in The Queen's heart, and she regards the role as its Head as of equal importance to being sovereign. For this reason, she has invariably made every effort to see all its member countries throughout her reign, particularly when they have something to celebrate. In July 1967, she was delighted to be in Canada to mark the country's centenary and open the festivities in Ottawa, the nation's capital; she also made a national broadcast expressing her concern that French-Canadian separatists wanted independence from the English-speaking majority.

In July 1969, two royal events took place that made history. The first was the showing of a film made for television, called *Royal Family*. This documentary enthralled first the nation and later the rest of the world; in Britain alone it was seen by 23 million viewers. It gave an unprecedented glimpse of the private side of The Queen and her family, and was an outstanding success, in spite of Her Majesty's initial instinctive reluctance to such exposure. (She revealed that her own first Christmas broadcast back in 1957 made her so nervous it practically spoiled her holiday.) She was eventually persuaded to agree, by Prince Philip and Lord Mountbatten, who were proved to be right. The film has rarely been shown since that first screening (the last being in 1977 as part of the Silver Jubilee celebrations) and Her Majesty has resisted all attempts to persuade her to allow it. However, the documentary would eventually open so many royal doors to other film and TV makers that perhaps Her Majesty was right in the first place.

ROYAL COMMAND PERFORMANCES

Throughout the decade, The Queen attended Command Performances and Royal Variety Shows, meeting the stars and producers. But she was never outshone by even the most glamorous stars, such as Marilyn Monroe and Frank Sinatra. Ever the diplomat, she always remains discreet about her own tastes. However, she was obviously delighted to meet Peter O'Toole after a Command Performance of *Lawrence of Arabia*, in which he starred, in 1962.

The Queen crowns her eldest son as Prince of Wales during his investiture ceremony at Caernarfon Castle.

On 1 July 1969, an even larger worldwide audience watched the investiture of Prince Charles as Prince of Wales at Caernarfon Castle. Organised by Lord Snowdon, the magnificent ceremony was a breathtaking spectacle narrated in both English and Welsh. A media circus with reporters from all over the world descended on the tiny Welsh town for weeks leading up to the ceremony, and there were thousands of people outside the castle when The Queen presented her son to his people as Prince of Wales.

In October 1971, Emperor Hirohito of Japan arrived in London for his first State Visit to Britain since before the Second World War. It was a controversial occasion because many former prisoners-of-war objected to the invitation, and The Queen acknowledged these feelings in her speech of welcome when she said: 'We cannot pretend that the past did not exist.' Lord Mountbatten declined an invitation to the State Banquet in honour of the Emperor. It was Mountbatten who had accepted the formal surrender of Japan in 1945 and he felt compelled to stand alongside his former comrades.

Emperor Hirohito and Empress Nagako of Japan with The Queen and other members of the Royal Family – including the Duke of Edinburgh, Duchess of Kent, Queen Mother, Duke of Kent, Prince Charles, Princess Anne, Lord Snowdon and Princess Margaret – at Buckingham Palace for a State Banquet in 1971.

THE 1960S

In 1961, Russian cosmonaut Yuri Gagarin became the first man in space, while eight years later, in 1969, American astronaut Neil Armstrong was the first man to walk on the moon. In the world of politics, in 1963 President of the United States John F. Kennedy was assassinated while on a visit to Texas; in 1965, Sir Winston Churchill, who served twice as Britain's Prime Minister, died at his London home. The Beatles had their first No.1 hit in the UK in 1963 with 'From Me To You'; The Rolling Stones' first No.1 came the following year with 'It's All Over Now'. That same year sporting legend Muhammad Ali won the World Heavyweight Boxing title and in 1966 Bobby Moore led the England football team to win the World Cup.

The Queen's Working Day

The Queen was brought up surrounded by protocol. There was a routine for everything and she was expected to obey the rules of the household from early childhood. She has become so used to having a regular routine that she would find it extraordinary if something was not in its place or if a meal, for example, was served when she didn't expect it. Even in her 90s, she likes her daily routine, described below, to be followed in exactly the same way as it always has, with no exceptions.

It is 7.30am and Buckingham Palace is starting to stir. The police sergeant sitting outside The Queen's bedroom (and wearing bedroom slippers) is coming to the end of his overnight shift. He used to go off duty at 6.30am, but after an intruder entered the royal bedroom at around 7am on the morning of 9 July 1982 – when no one was on guard – the extra hour was added. Her Majesty's personal maid walks towards him carrying the 'morning tray' for her royal mistress. On it are solid-silver

Princess Elizabeth and Princess Margaret were raised with the familiarity of formal protocol; here, watched by their parents, the young sisters step forward to shake hands on arriving at the Royal Tournament at Olympia in London in 1936.

pots of Earl Grey tea and hot water, cold milk but no sugar. The cup and saucer are of bone china and there is also a fine linen napkin draped across the tray which bears the royal cypher EIIR. The maid gives a light tap on the door, which bears the legend 'The Queen' on a white card in a plain brass holder. Without waiting to be called she enters the room and walks quietly across to the bedside table with its family photographs and telephone, complete with 'panic button' – the one which was so spectacularly ignored on the morning when Michael Fagan became the only man – apart from her husband – to see The Queen asleep in bed.

Her Majesty's large double bed has white linen sheets, measuring 80 x 112 inches (200 x 285cm) and bearing the monogram HM The Queen, exactly 3½ inches (9cm) high, and featherdown pillows complete with lace border and the same monogram, but this time a more modest 1½ inches (4cm) high.

The colour scheme of the room is pale green, which is The Queen's favourite shade. Putting the tray down, the maid then switches on the radio, always tuned to BBC Radio 4 as Her Majesty likes to wake up to the sound of the day's early news.

ABOVE: Bearing the royal cypher, bone-china tableware designed in celebration of The Queen's Silver Jubilee.

RIGHT: The royal cypher on a village postbox.

Quite often The Queen, an early riser, is already awake; she bids her maid 'good morning' and asks what the weather outside looks like. Then, while Her Majesty is enjoying her first cup of tea, her maid will go into the adjoining bathroom to draw the bath, which has to be exactly the right temperature; it is tested with a thermometer, and no more than 7 inches (18cm) of water fills the royal bathtub.

While the Queen is bathing, one of her three dressers lays out the first outfit of the day in the adjacent dressing room with its floor-to-ceiling mirrors and walk-in wardrobes. The dresser knows exactly what is needed as she was given The Queen's daily programme the evening before. Depending on the engagements for the day, Her Majesty may have to change as many as five times, but she rarely makes her own choice; she says that is what she pays her dressers for. The dresser removes the clothes The Queen has worn the night before, and each article is examined and brushed before being returned to its place in one of the giant wardrobes on the floor above. The wardrobe secretary lists the date and occasion each garment has been worn, for future reference.

In 2016, the exhibition *Fashioning a Reign: 90 Years of Style from The Queen's Wardrobe* was on display at Buckingham Palace. Shown here (left to right): Princess Elizabeth's wartime ATS uniform; a 1958 blue and gold evening dress by Sir Norman Hartnell (who made both Her Majesty's wedding dress and Coronation gown); a turquoise shift dress with silver embroidery by Hardy Amies, worn by Her Majesty for an official portrait taken by Cecil Beaton in 1968; another outfit by Hartnell, this one worn by The Queen at the wedding of Princess Anne to Mark Phillips in 1973; and the pale primrose hat and coat designed by Angela Kelly, worn by Her Majesty at the wedding of Prince William and Catherine Middleton in 2011.

Once The Queen has dressed, her hairdresser brushes and arranges her hair in the style that hasn't changed in decades. Breakfast is served promptly at 8.30am in The Queen's private dining room. A footman has brought the food to a hotplate – a silver 'muffin dish' with the food on top and hot water underneath – and once he has served it, he leaves the room so Her Majesty can eat in peace.

As with everything The Queen uses, the breakfast utensils are of the best quality: the cutlery solid silver, the crockery Sevres bone china and even the butter imprinted with the royal cypher. The milk will have been delivered early that morning from the royal dairy at Windsor, in bottles again bearing the royal cypher. Her Majesty is said to have once remarked that the first time she really realised she was Queen was when she saw those milk bottles with EIIR on them.

By 9.30am the Queen will be seated at her desk in her sitting room-cum-office, ready for two solid hours of paperwork. The room is comfortable rather than luxurious, with armchairs and sofas upholstered in country-house-style chintz. The Chinese carpet is another shade of green. The room is very much as it was in the King's day and, like his daughter, George VI preferred this colour to any other. Much earlier that morning the palace florist arrived to arrange fresh flowers which are in profusion around the room. The Chippendale desk is the one The Queen brought with her when she moved from her earlier home at Clarence House in 1952. It is cluttered with personal treasures and family photographs, including one of the Queen Mother taken during the Second World War, and another of 'Grannie' – old Queen Mary. There is also a favourite small leather-framed folding album showing a young, smiling Princess Elizabeth and Prince Philip. A heavy crystal double inkwell contains the black ink which The Queen uses to sign official documents and the special green ink she likes to use for personal letters. She rarely uses a ballpoint pen, insisting on her favourite old fountain pen with a heavy gold nib. There is also a pristine sheet of blotting paper (destroyed every day), black in colour so that no one can see what has been written should they hold it up to a mirror. A leather folder, again with the royal crest, contains Her Majesty's stationery; there is a sponge for dampening envelopes and memo pads for writing notes to her staff.

The Queen at work at her desk in 1959, surrounded by family photographs.

The Queen's press secretary will have already clipped any items of interest from all the morning newspapers and prepared a digest of the day's news from the early morning radio and television bulletins. Once Her Majesty has read these and any other papers she might need to see, she presses a button on the console in front of her, which connects her directly with several members of her household. Later in the morning, the duty lady-in-waiting is called into the sitting room. The Queen shows her some letters which require a personal reply. Those from children and the elderly get special attention, and the lady-in-waiting writes the letters and signs them on behalf of The Queen. Personal friends who write to Her Majesty put their initials in the lower left-hand corner of the envelope and when the staff see these they know they are not to open them, for The Queen likes to open her personal mail herself.

In the early days of The Queen's reign, the royal chef would arrive in Her Majesty's quarters at the start of the week with a complete list of suggestions – including three alternatives – for every meal over the coming seven days. The Queen would tick those she preferred, occasionally making choices of her own. These days the system is basically the same, except that the chef does not come upstairs in person. Instead he sends the list to Her Majesty's page, who returns it when The Queen has indicated what she wants. Even so, she still knows on Monday what she is having for dinner on Thursday, and all menus continue to be written in French.

The Queen has adapted to modern technology in a manner that would have mystified her parents and horrified her grandparents. She has a personal mobile and has learned how to text; her handset is among the most sophisticated in the world. It is encrypted (just like the one used by James Bond) and said to be impossible to be hacked into. Apparently, she was given personal instruction on how to operate it

The Queen is adept at using all sorts of 21st-century technology; this photograph of her using a laptop was taken in 2002 during a visit to New Brunswick, Canada, as part of her Golden Jubilee tour of the Commonwealth, where Her Majesty opened the new Sussex Elementary School.

The Queen with Princess Michael of Kent (far left), Her Majesty's racing manager John Warren (second left) and the Earl and Countess of Wessex at Epsom Racecourse on Derby Day, 2012.

by her granddaughter Zara Tindall, who, like most of her generation, is a whizz with technical gadgets. The Queen also possesses an iPod, a tablet, a laptop – and she's on Facebook, but nobody outside of Buckingham Palace knows how many 'Friends' she has admitted. The royal mobile is kept fully charged at all times by The Queen's personal assistant. It's an ultra-slim model complete with camera facility, small and light enough to fit into a pocket or handbag.

The two people Her Majesty speaks to most frequently on the phone are her daughter and her racing manager, John Warren, the son-in-law of The Queen's former racing manager and great friend, the late Earl of Carnarvon, whose home was Highclere Castle, known to many television viewers as Downton Abbey. And when The Queen woke early in the morning of 9 July 1982 to find an intruder, Michael Fagan, sitting on her bed at Buckingham Palace, the first call she made afterwards was to her daughter, Anne.

The telephone exchange at Buckingham Palace is situated on the ground floor, near the Guard Room, and is manned by females during the daytime and men throughout the night, a custom that dates back to the early days of telephones at the palace. It never closes; 24 hours a day, 365 days a year, when The Queen lifts her telephone to speak to an operator she is always answered within two seconds. And when she asks for a call to be made she invariably makes it sound like a request. The exchange is said to have the best directory in the world, possessing the private numbers of every world leader and anyone else who needs to be contacted, and The Queen is known to speak on the telephone regularly with leaders of the Commonwealth countries.

Her Majesty made her first transatlantic telephone call as sovereign early in 1952 when she spoke with President Harry S. Truman at the White House, and the following year, Coronation year, she talked with his successor, President Dwight D. Eisenhower, who she had known as General Eisenhower during the years of the Second World War. Today, Buckingham Palace and Clarence House would not be able to function without the telephone, and The Queen and Prince Charles would find it very strange indeed if they could not lift the phone and be connected immediately with someone anywhere in the world.

Around 30 times a year an investiture is held in the palace Ballroom, or in the Waterloo Chamber at Windsor Castle, when some 60 men and women receive their honours from The Queen, or from the Prince of Wales, Prince William or The Princess Royal. The ceremony starts promptly at midday and lasts exactly one hour. The Queen has performed this particular royal duty hundreds of times, yet she still manages to make it appear as if it is the first time for her also, and that she is enjoying the occasion as much as the recipients.

D-Day veteran Harry Billinge was made an MBE (Member of the Order of the British Empire) by The Queen during an investiture ceremony at Buckingham Palace in 2020.

Immediately after lunch, The Queen likes to walk in the gardens with her dogs. Household staff know they should keep well out of the way at this time. Only the gardeners may remain, and they speak only if first addressed by Her Majesty. All afternoon engagements are scheduled to finish before 4.30 so that the Queen can be back at the palace in time for tea at 5pm. It's an immovable feast and the meal she enjoys the most: tiny sandwiches cut to precise size and without crusts; warm scones with cream and strawberry jam; and, always, her favourite Dundee fruitcake. The ritual never changes and neither does the fare. However, Her Majesty doesn't eat the scones herself; they are ordered solely for the dogs.

CORGIS AND DORGIS

Her Majesty has owned over 30 corgi dogs, starting with Susan in 1944. Today she is left with only two, but she also had a 'dorgi', a cross between a corgi and dachshund. When she was asked how two such short dogs could mate, she is reported to have replied, while keeping a straight face, 'We stand one of them on a brick.' True or false? Either way it's a great story and one that has entered royal legend.

The Queen's corgis got in on the act when the New Zealand All Blacks rugby team met Her Majesty at Buckingham Palace on 5 November 2002. The team had travelled to Europe for a series of matches against England, Wales and France.

The Queen and Prime Minister Boris Johnson at a weekly meeting at Buckingham Palace, June 2021; this was their first face-to-face audience following the start of the Covid-19 pandemic.

For the rest of the day, The Queen continues the daily round of work as industriously as ever. Visitors are received and entertained, private correspondence is attended to, and the Prime Minister is given an audience every Tuesday evening at 6.30 to report on important domestic and international issues. The Privy Council meets, on average, once a month – and still conducts all its business while its members (including The Queen) are standing, following a tradition first instituted during Queen Victoria's reign – so that the Royal Assent can be given to government legislation. The demands of being a constitutional monarch are unrelenting, and Her Majesty is a perfect example of a working sovereign. For her, the work never ends.

Having started work at 9.30am, she rarely leaves her desk before 6pm, and even then she is required to attend to her 'boxes' containing the communications, official papers, documents and telegrams from various government departments, which have to be read and initialled every day.

It is not only at Buckingham Palace that The Queen spends the day working; here she is photographed at Balmoral in 1972, attending to papers from the red despatch box that require the attention of the Head of State. These red despatch boxes, used by Members of Parliament and the monarch, have become an iconic symbol of British government.

The Queen's arrival is heralded at an evening reception for the Diplomatic Corps at Buckingham Palace in 2019.

If there is no evening engagement, The Queen retires to her own rooms to rest before changing for dinner. The exception is on Tuesday evenings, when the Prime Minister arrives for the weekly audience at 6.30. It used to be an hour earlier, but when Prince Charles and Princess Anne were small, their mother liked to spend that time with them so she changed the appointment to 6.30pm – and it has remained so ever since. The meeting is official, so takes place in the Audience Room, on the north-west corner between the Royal Closet and The Queen's dining room, and lasts for no more than half an hour.

Her Majesty is not a late-night person. She is usually in bed by 11pm, where she likes to read. She has always been sent the first edition of every equestrian thriller by Dick Francis (now written by his son Felix). So, often, the last lights seen shining out of the north side of Buckingham Palace are those in The Queen's rooms. They are easy to identify; they are the only ones with bow windows, overlooking Constitution Hill. And tomorrow, if it's a working day, The Queen will follow precisely the same routine. It is what she is used to, so why change it?

The Third Decade: 1972–1981

In most years of her reign The Queen has made State Visits abroad, making her by far the most widely travelled monarch in British history. The decade saw the first State Visit by a British monarch to a Communist country when The Queen visited Yugoslavia in October 1972. During the 1977 Silver Jubilee Tour of the South Pacific, a roof collapsed in Fiji in the middle of some local dances to welcome the royal visitors. Once The Queen had been assured that nobody was hurt, she took advantage of the crowd running to the scene by discreetly sneaking her lipstick out of her handbag and checking her make-up. It was a nice human touch to an otherwise stiff and rigid engagement.

A year before Britain joined the EEC in 1973, The Queen and Prince Philip celebrated their Silver Wedding anniversary, 25 years of a very happy and successful marriage.

The Queen and Prince Philip at Balmoral in 1972, the year that they celebrated their Silver Wedding anniversary.

The society wedding of 1973 was that between Princess Anne and Mark Phillips. It was a State occasion with thousands of guests inside Westminster Abbey and seen by 500 million people on television worldwide. There could not be a greater contrast to Princess Anne's second wedding, in 1992, to Tim (now Vice-Admiral Sir Timothy) Laurence, which was held at Crathie Kirk, a tiny parish church near the Balmoral Estate in Scotland, attended by only 30 guests and with no photographers allowed inside the church.

The Queen was deeply saddened in July 1978 when her sister, Princess Margaret, divorced her husband, the Earl of Snowdon, although Her Majesty remained on the best of terms with Lord Snowdon until he died in 2017. The following month, Her Majesty and Prince Philip were accompanied by Prince Andrew and Prince Edward when they attended the Commonwealth Games in Edmonton, Canada.

It was during this decade that three new Prime Ministers took office: Harold Wilson in 1974, James Callaghan in 1976 and Margaret Thatcher, who became

PETER AND ZARA PHILLIPS

Princess Anne and Mark Phillips have two children: Peter, The Queen's first grandchild, was born on 15 November 1977 and his sister Zara on 15 May 1981. Peter married a Canadian woman, Autumn Kelly, but they divorced in 2021, after having two children, Savannah and Isla. Zara is married to England rugby international Mike Tindall; their children are Mia, Lena and Lucas.

Britain's first female Prime Minister in 1979. This was also the year when the Royal Family suffered a devastating blow. Prince Philip's Uncle 'Dickie', Earl Mountbatten of Burma, had been sailing with his family off the coast of Ireland, near his holiday home at Classiebawn Castle. It was August Bank Holiday Monday when Mountbatten, together with several member of his family and a young local boy, set out in their fishing boat, *Shadow V*. Minutes later, a bomb was exploded by remote control, operated by two members of the IRA. Lord Mountbatten was killed instantly, together with one of his grandsons and the young Irish boy; the rest of the group were injured and Mountbatten's son-in-law's mother died from her injuries the next day. The Queen and Prince Philip were the first to be informed. As with all such occasions, the Royal Household swung into immediate action to prepare for the funeral. The Queen decided that although it was not to be a full State Funeral it was to be a full ceremonial occasion – in other words a hero's farewell, to be held at Westminster Abbey on 5 September 1979. It was a fitting tribute to the man who had survived being torpedoed during the Second World War.

In March 1981, The Queen met with members of the Privy Council, including Prime Minister Margaret Thatcher (seated, second left), at Buckingham Palace to confer on the proposed marriage of Prince Charles and Lady Diana Spencer.

The Queen, dressed in a long black taffeta gown, during her State Visit to the Vatican in 1980; at her meeting with the Pope, described as 'warm and relaxed', Her Majesty spoke of her assurances of sincere friendship and goodwill.

A truly historic visit took place in 1980 when The Queen became the first British monarch to make a State Visit to the Vatican, meeting with Pope John Paul II; she made a return visit exactly 20 years later.

As this decade of Her Majesty's reign drew to a close, she was involved in some high drama. In June 1981, as she was riding her horse Burmese to the annual Trooping the Colour Parade, a youth fired six shots at her – only later found to be blanks. Her Majesty successfully controlled her mount and continued with the ceremony as if nothing had happened, a remarkable tribute to her own self-discipline.

The following month saw the spectacular and widely televised marriage of Prince Charles and Lady Diana Spencer at St Paul's Cathedral. They chose the cathedral instead of the traditional Westminster Abbey because by doing so they were able to invite over 500 more guests.

PRINCES WILLIAM AND HARRY

Charles and Diana – the Prince and Princess of Wales – had two children. The first, Prince William (now Duke of Cambridge), was born on 21 June 1982. He married Catherine Middleton in 2011 and they have three children: Prince George, Princess Charlotte and Prince Louis. Charles and Diana's second son, Prince Harry (now Duke of Sussex), was born on 15 September 1984. He married American actress Meghan Markle in 2018 and they have two children: Archie and Lilibet.

The Royal Family and wedding guests pose with Prince Charles and Lady Diana following their marriage ceremony on 29 July 1981.

In December 1981, The Queen found herself in the unusual position of having to seek refuge in an English pub. As The Queen was being driven back to Windsor after a visit to Princess Anne's home in Gloucestershire, a sudden snowstorm caused her car to be stranded in waist-high drifts, and the startled landlord of the nearest pub – the Cross Hands on the edge of the Cotswolds – suddenly found himself acting as host to the sovereign for several hours, having first thought it was a hoax. A plaque at the pub marks the occasion.

THE 1970S

In 1970, Paul McCartney announced the break-up of the Beatles. The following year, Idi Amin seized power in Uganda. In 1973, Britain joined the EEC (European Economic Community) and the year after the Conservative Government of Edward Heath collapsed. In 1976, Bjorn Borg won his first Wimbledon tennis men's single champion title, an achievement repeated for five consecutive years until being defeated by John McEnroe in 1981. Elvis Presley, nicknamed the 'King of Rock 'n' Roll', died in Memphis, Tennessee in 1977, at the age of 42. Two years later Margaret Thatcher became Britain's first-ever female Prime Minister.

The Fourth Decade: 1982–1991

On 21 June 1982, Prince William, The Queen's grandson and future king, was born to Prince Charles and Princess Diana. He was the first child born to a Prince and Princess of Wales since 1905, and his birth ensured the continuity of the royal line of succession for the foreseeable future.

Pope John Paul II arrived at Buckingham Palace in May of that year, becoming the first Pope to visit Britain for 450 years. Several members of the Royal Household later said the Pope was the most impressive figure that Her Majesty had ever met.

Also in 1982, The Queen took the opportunity to combine a visit to Australia – for the Commonwealth Games in Brisbane – with a tour of several of the smaller countries in the South Pacific, including Papua New Guinea, the Solomon Islands, Nauru, Kiribati, Tuvalu and Fiji. She has always believed her responsibilities to the Commonwealth are as equally important as her duties to the United Kingdom.

Riding in Windsor Great Park in 1982: The Queen on her horse Burmese and US President Ronald Reagan on Centennial.

A number of Presidents of the United States became friends of The Queen and Prince Philip, perhaps none more so than the late President Ronald Reagan. In 1982, he was a guest of The Queen at Windsor Castle, and they took the opportunity of horse riding together in Windsor Great Park. The following year President Reagan returned the compliment when he acted as host to Her Majesty during her visit to California.

In 1986, Prince Andrew married Sarah Ferguson and The Queen made him Duke of York. Although Prince Andrew and his wife, known as Fergie, divorced in 1996, they have stayed the best of friends.

It was in 1986 that The Queen became the first British monarch to visit China. During this historic event she and the Duke of Edinburgh walked along the Great Wall, where Her Majesty insisted on taking her own photographs with

PRINCESSES BEATRICE AND EUGENIE

The Duke and Duchess of York have two children: Princess Beatrice, born 9 August 1988, was married in 2020 and has a daughter, Sienna Elizabeth Mapelli Mozzi; Princess Eugenie, born 23 March 1990, was married in 2018 and has a son, August Philip Hawke Brooksbank.

a camera she had brought along specially to record the occasion. This was also the year that she celebrated her 60th birthday.

A year later, The Queen bestowed the title of The Princess Royal on her only daughter, Anne. This, the rarest of all royal titles, had been vacant since the death of Princess Mary, the only daughter of King George V, in 1965, and Princess Anne is only the seventh woman ever to hold the position. The honour was seen as recognition of the unflagging public service the Princess had given – and continues to give – over many years. The title is in The Queen's gift and she does not have to seek advice from anyone regarding its bestowal. Her Majesty wanted to elevate Anne to a unique place in Court precedence as previously she had been lower than those ladies senior to her, solely because they had married one of the princes.

ABOVE: The Queen and Princess Anne have always had a shared love of horses; here, on holiday at Balmoral in 1955, mother and daughter adjust the bridle of one of the royal ponies, named Greensleeves.

LEFT: The Queen and Prince Philip at the Great Wall of China in 1986.

In 1990, John Major became Prime Minister as the new leader of the Conservative party, following the departure of Margaret Thatcher. The Queen has never even given a hint of who she might regard as her favourite Prime Ministers. Many people imagine that because of her class and status she might be a natural Conservative. However, Harold Wilson and James Callaghan, both Labour, were known to be on the best of terms with Her Majesty, and Callaghan (later Lord Callaghan of Cardiff) revealed that occasionally, at the Tuesday audience, he and The Queen would end up discussing their respective gardens. Mrs Thatcher, on the other hand, at first found it intimidating to meet The Queen in this capacity, but eventually they reached an understanding and remained cordial throughout their relationship.

The glitter of the younger members of the Royal Family, such as the Prince and Princess of Wales and the Duke and Duchess of York, complemented the grace of The Queen and the enthusiasm of the Duke of Edinburgh when they all visited Australia – at different times – to help celebrate the country's bicentenary in 1988. Her Majesty performed the opening ceremony of the new Parliament House in Canberra, describing the vast building on Capital Hill as a 'symbol of Australian unity and democracy'.

Her Majesty's early enthusiasm for foreign travel has never fully dimmed, and when she received an invitation to visit Iceland for the first time in June 1990, she was delighted to accept. The reception she received from the thousands who welcomed her was amongst the warmest and friendliest she had ever known.

The special relationship between Britain and the United States was exemplified in May 1991 when The Queen became the first British Head of State to address a joint meeting of the US Congress in Washington DC. It was a triumphant moment which demonstrated the true value of Her Majesty as a ceremonial ambassador. As she stood at the podium and started her speech, she commented, 'I do hope you can see me from where you are.' She was referring to an incident the previous day at the White House welcoming ceremony; the previous speaker, much taller than Her Majesty, had forgotten to adjust the microphone to The Queen's height and only her hat was visible to the audience. Her little joke broke the ice completely and she had the combined audience of Democrats and Republicans in the palm of her hand.

Later that year, in October, The Queen attended the Commonwealth Heads of Government Conference in Zimbabwe and met Nelson Mandela, who, the previous year, had been released after being imprisoned for 27 years. Her Majesty was now by

Her Majesty The Queen had the audience in the palm of her hand when she cracked a joke at the joint meeting of the US Congress in Washington DC, 16 May 1991.

far the most experienced Head of State in the world; on her many overseas visits, the ministers and diplomats who accompanied her were proud of the way in which she supported their official business dealings with their opposite numbers, without in any way relinquishing her own pivotal role as sovereign.

THE 1980S

Former Beatle John Lennon was murdered in New York in 1980. In 1982, the Falklands Campaign began when Argentina invaded the islands; Prince Andrew saw active service as a Royal Navy helicopter pilot during the conflict. In 1985, the first mobile phone call was made in Britain and in 1987 work began on the long-awaited Channel Tunnel. World tragedies during this decade included the Lockerbie Pan Am bombing in 1988 and the following year, in China, the Tiananmen Square massacre took place.

LEFT: Prince Edward and Sophie Rhys-Jones were married on 19 June 1999. The ceremony took place at St George's Chapel, Windsor Castle.

OPPOSITE: The Queen at Royal Ascot in 1995; the prestigious race meeting is understood to be one of Her Majesty's favourite events of the year.

The Fifth Decade: 1992–2001

As the reign of Elizabeth II entered its fifth decade, The Queen remained uncompromisingly regal, the model of stability in a changing world. The devolving of some political powers to Wales and Scotland saw her attending the opening sessions of the Welsh Assembly in May 1999 and the new Scottish Parliament in July that year.

In June of the same year, she had attended the wedding of her youngest son, Prince Edward, to Sophie Rhys-Jones; on that day he was created Earl of Wessex.

LADY LOUISE WINDSOR AND JAMES, VISCOUNT SEVERN

The Earl and Duchess of Wessex have two children: Lady Louise Windsor, born 8 November 2003, and James, Viscount Severn, born 17 December 2007.

Part of the decade was taken up with the aftermath of the dramatic fire that swept through Windsor Castle on 20 November 1992, the 45th wedding anniversary of The Queen and Prince Philip. Although many priceless works of art were salvaged, nine of the finest State Apartments were damaged or destroyed, including St George's Hall. Prince Andrew helped to rescue some of the priceless works of art as the fire ripped through 115 rooms and caused over £36 million worth of damage. The Queen was closely involved in the task of restoration, which began almost immediately and was completed five years later. The State Apartments, restored by a superb combination of ancient crafts and modern technology, could at last be reopened to the public.

It was appropriate that St George's Hall, magnificently brought back to its original splendour, should be the scene of the party to celebrate the 50th anniversary of the royal couple's wedding in 1997. Theirs had been an enduring partnership based on mutual love, trust and understanding, with Prince Philip acknowledged as The Queen's staunchest supporter – or, as she herself described him, 'My rock'.

This decade brought with it some shocks and sadness for The Queen. The marriages of both the Prince and Princess of Wales and the Duke and Duchess of York broke down irretrievably, and later came the tragic and untimely death of the Princess of Wales in 1997, which saw The Queen providing support initially to her family and then to her people as they mourned the loss of this popular public figure. The death of Diana, Princess of Wales on 31 August 1997, unleashed a tide of public grief on an unprecedented scale, a virtual tsunami of sadness throughout the world. She was 36 years old and nobody was prepared for the shock of losing this beautiful,

TRANSPORT HISTORY

On 6 May 1994, The Queen made transport history when she and Prince Philip travelled through the Channel Tunnel from London to Calais on the newly opened Eurostar railway. The journey from England to France took precisely 32 minutes.

The Queen and Prince Philip are greeted by President François Mitterrand as they arrive in Calais following their first trip on Eurostar for the inauguration ceremony.

A fire began on the morning of 20 November 1992 and swept through Windsor Castle; it was not until the early hours of the next day that the final secondary fires were extinguished.

The Queen is greeted by the Dean of Westminster, Wesley Carr, as she arrives at Westminster Abbey for the funeral of Diana, Princess of Wales, on 6 September 1997.

vibrant young woman in the prime of her life. She appeared to have everything to live for, in spite of the fact that she had been involved in one of the most acrimonious divorces of the century, and suffered the humiliation of being stripped of what many people believed to be her rightful style of Her Royal Highness.

Diana made no secret of the fact that the role she considered to be the most important in her life was raising her two sons. They were her number one priority and everything else was secondary to their welfare. And, had she survived, she would have been a proud and loving grandmother to Prince William's children, George, Charlotte and Louis, and Prince Harry's children, Archie and Lilibet.

Diana had that elusive star quality which she managed to combine with the common touch. Ordinary men, women and children felt they could approach her without any fear of being rebuffed; in fact, she encouraged people to talk to her – and even touch her – no matter what their background. One of The Queen's ladies-in-waiting explained Diana's tactile approach, saying she was a natural 'hugger and kisser'.

The year 1997 brought one of the few occasions when The Queen was seen to wipe away a tear in public. The reason was the loss of her beloved Royal Yacht *Britannia*, the ship she called her 'home from home'. Her Majesty had launched the yacht in April 1953 and on its maiden voyage it had carried Prince Charles and Princess Anne to Malta, to be reunited with their parents towards the end of their Coronation tour in 1954. *Britannia* had hosted four royal honeymoons: Princess Margaret and

Lord Snowdon in 1960, Princess Anne and Mark Phillips in 1973, the Prince and Princess of Wales in 1981, and the Duke and Duchess of York in 1986. As all four marriages ended in divorce, the yacht's nickname of 'The Love Boat' could hardly be said to be appropriate. *Britannia*'s final voyage saw the handing over of Hong Kong to China, so this was, perhaps, a fitting end to a magnificent maritime career. And it was at the final decommissioning ceremony in Portsmouth that tears were seen in The Queen's eyes. *Britannia* now lies in a permanent berth at Leith in Scotland and is a popular visitor attraction.

But if that was one of the saddest occasions, few could compare with the happiness that surrounded the Royal Family on 4 August 2000. The reason? It was the 100th birthday of Queen Elizabeth the Queen Mother, who had lived through six reigns and two world wars in a century that had also seen a man walk on the moon. It was a fitting climax to a period of high drama, intense sadness and great joy. The following year, it was The Queen's aunt, Princess Alice, Duchess of Gloucester, who celebrated her 100th birthday on 25 December 2001.

Towards the end of the decade, The Queen was at the Millennium Stadium in Wales to present the Rugby Union World Cup to the winners, Australia. Shortly before the event, she learned that, in a referendum, Australia had voted to retain her as its Head of State. It must have given her a moment of quiet gratification to know that after nearly 50 years she was still held in such affection by many of her people who live half a world away.

The Queen and Prince Philip attended the decommissioning of the Royal Yacht *Britannia* on 11 December 1997.

In July 2000, The Queen Mother, accompanied by Prince Charles, arrives for a pageant on Horse Guards Parade as part of her 100th birthday celebrations.

THE 1990S

In 1990 the Berlin Wall was finally demolished and in 1994 Nelson Mandela became President of South Africa. On a financial front, the following year the centuries-old Barings Bank collapsed. A happier event in 1995 saw three royal ladies, The Queen, Queen Elizabeth the Queen Mother and Princess Margaret, standing on the balcony at Buckingham Palace, while below nearly 500,000 people waved and cheered. The occasion was the 50th anniversary of the ending of the Second World War in Europe; it was a proud and moving moment, and one that proved yet again that for the people of Britain, Buckingham Palace becomes the focal point in times of great celebration and emotion. In fact a time of great emotion and a national outpouring of grief came in 1997 with the untimely death of Diana, Princess of Wales in a car crash. In 1999, devolution arrived in Scotland with the opening of the first Scottish Parliament in 300 years.

The Sixth Decade: 2002–2011

This decade began on a note of double tragedy for The Queen. In February 2002, Princess Margaret died. Then, in March, the Queen Mother died, having reached the grand old age of 101.

Princess Margaret had endured ill health for several years. A heavy smoker since her teens, and her love of partying and the excesses that went with it, all took their toll. She had suffered a series of strokes and at exactly 6.30 on the morning of 9 February 2002 she died at King Edward VII's Hospital in London, just one day after another stroke caused cardiac problems. She had discussed with her sister, The Queen, what arrangements there should be for her funeral and it was agreed that a private family service, with just a few close friends, should be held at St George's Chapel in Windsor Castle. It took place on 15 February 2002. But, unlike nearly every other member of the Royal Family before her, she was not buried in one of

the royal vaults but cremated at Slough Crematorium and her ashes brought back to Windsor, to lie in the King George VI Memorial Chapel. Memorial services were held at St Mary Magdalene Church at Sandringham and also at Glamis Castle, where Princess Margaret had been born.

Seven weeks later came another blow for The Queen, but one that was not entirely unexpected. The Queen Mother died in her sleep at 3.15 on the afternoon of 30 March 2002, Easter Saturday. She was at her country residence, Royal Lodge in Windsor Great Park, with her daughter, The Queen, at her bedside. Every member of the Royal Family has a code name relating to their death, and at once Operation Tay Bridge, the code name for the Queen Mother's funeral, was brought into action.

The Queen Mother was brought to Westminster Hall where she lay in state for three days. Over 200,000 people filed past her coffin, which was guarded by troops – and at certain times by male members of the Royal Family.

It was hard to believe that just a few short weeks earlier the Queen Mother had attended the funeral of her younger daughter, Princess Margaret; she had been in a wheelchair as she had suffered a bad fall but refused to allow photographers to take any pictures of her in it.

The Queen Mother's funeral was attended by foreign royalty and the leaders or their representatives of nearly every country in the world. Buckingham Palace received more than 30,000 messages of condolence.

On a happier note, on 9 April 2005 Prince Charles married Mrs Camilla Parker Bowles. His Royal Highness had to make a formal request to The Queen, even before he proposed to Camilla. This was a requirement under the Royal Marriages Act of 1772, which states that any lineal descendant of George II must obtain the

The Queen and Prince Charles walk behind the Queen Mother's coffin following her funeral service at Westminster Abbey on 9 April 2002.

Prince Charles and his bride, Camilla, pictured with their parents and children in the White Drawing Room at Windsor Castle on their wedding day, 9 April 2005.

consent of the sovereign in order to marry. Prince William and Prince Harry were told of their father's engagement several weeks before the news was made public. They both expressed their pleasure, later issuing a joint statement: 'We are both very happy for our father and Camilla and we wish them all the luck in the future.'

It was a second marriage for both Charles and Camilla, and as they were both divorced the difficulties with the Church of England forced them to have a civil marriage service at Windsor's Guildhall. This was followed immediately by a service of blessing at St George's Chapel, Windsor, by the then Archbishop of Canterbury, Dr Rowan Williams. Camilla assumed the subsidiary title of Duchess of Cornwall, not Princess of Wales, to which she is legally entitled. And if and when Prince Charles ascends the throne it is anticipated that she will be crowned alongside him as Queen.

THE 2000S

The decade began with news of the crash of Concorde in Paris; all passengers and crew were killed and it was an event that heralded the end of the first supersonic commercial air services. In 2001, the Twin Towers in New York were attacked by terrorists, killing nearly 3,000 people. In 2002, the euro currency made its first appearance. That year Her Majesty celebrated her Golden Jubilee, marking her half-century on the throne; as part of the celebrations, at the Party in the Park concert Brian May of rock group Queen played a guitar solo of 'God Save The Queen' from the roof of Buckingham Palace. In 2006, Saddam Hussain was executed for crimes against humanity. A year later the American company Apple introduced the first iPhone. In 2009, music icon Michael Jackson died, aged 50, at his home in Los Angeles.

The Seventh Decade: 2012–2021

This was to turn out to be a bumper decade for royal marriages. On 29 April 2011, the wedding took place between Prince William and Catherine Middleton, and on the day they were married The Queen created William Duke of Cambridge, Earl of Strathearn and Baron Carrickfergus. It truly was a fairy-tale occasion, proving that, even amongst royalty, where true love blossoms one's origins do not matter. The new Duchess was born into a middle-class family and educated at Marlborough College, one of the country's most exclusive – and expensive – public schools. From there she went to the equally prestigious University of St Andrews, where she first encountered her future husband. The days when royalty married only royalty were long gone, never to return.

The Duchess of Cambridge had come from a stable background that gave William a rare glimpse of what a normal family life could be. He loved it. Of course,

On 29 April 2011, their families gather on the balcony at Buckingham Palace as Prince William and his bride, Catherine Middleton, share a kiss, to the great delight of the thousands gathered in The Mall to see them.

William's life had been mapped out from the moment he was born. Everything he has done has been planned with an eye on his future role as King: the job for which he will be the only applicant and for which he will be the best qualified.

Catherine's transformation from commoner to royal Duchess (and Princess) began on the very day she and William were married at Westminster Abbey by the then Archbishop of Canterbury, Dr Rowan Williams. William's brother, Prince Harry, was the best man, or 'supporter' as they are called in royal circles. William and Catherine adhered to Royal Family tradition by choosing wedding rings made from Welsh gold. As the couple walked back down the aisle at the end of the service, they paused to bow and curtsey to The Queen.

Her Majesty paid for the wedding, as she has for all her children and grandchildren, and there were 650 guests at the wedding breakfast at Buckingham Palace. In fact there were two receptions; the second was held in the evening at Clarence House, to which William drove Catherine in his father's classic convertible Aston Martin – complete with L-plates attached. It was a wonderful start to what has proved to be a happy and highly successful marriage, blessed with, as we now know, the birth of three children.

A few months later, Her Majesty was delighted when her granddaughter Zara Phillips married England rugby international Mike Tindall in Edinburgh, where the ceremony was attended by a galaxy of celebrities from the worlds of sport and show business.

St George's Chapel in the grounds of Windsor Castle was the scene of possibly the most anticipated wedding of the time. On 19 May 2018, Prince Harry married American actress Meghan Markle in a spectacular ceremony; 600 guests attended the service, including many luminaries from the world of music, film and sport. It was the first time a person of mixed-race ancestry had joined the Royal Family and she was warmly welcomed by her new relatives.

Meghan was accompanied by her mother, Doria Raglan, as her father, Thomas Markle, was unwell. Meghan elected to walk up the steps leading to the chapel alone, but as she walked down the aisle to join Prince Harry, she was met by her future father-in-law, the Prince of Wales, who offered his arm and stood in for her father. And at the conclusion of the ceremony, the Prince of Wales again displayed perfect chivalry by offering his arm to Meghan's mother when he and his wife, the Duchess of Cornwall, left their stall.

The Queen made Harry Duke of Sussex, Earl of Dumbarton and Baron Kilkeel, so Meghan also received three titles to add to her name that day. As is their style, the couple had requested that, instead of wedding presents, their guests should donate to charities.

The couple were given the lease of Frogmore Cottage at Windsor, which they made their home. However, less than two years after the wedding came the decision that not only saddened the Royal Family but shocked the nation. The Duke and

Prince Harry and his bride, Meghan Markle, leave St George's Chapel after their wedding ceremony, which took place on 19 May 2018.

Duchess of Sussex announced that they did not wish to carry out royal duties and were relocating to California, as private citizens. The Queen took the unprecedented step of issuing a personal statement saying that Harry and Meghan would no longer be working members of the Royal Family and would not be permitted to use the style His (or Her) Royal Highness for their commercial activities. Harry was also ordered to give up his royal patronages, including being Captain General of the Royal Marines, a post previously held by his grandfather, Prince Philip. The couple opted to retain Frogmore Cottage as a British base, for which Harry is said to pay a 'commercial rent' and for which he has repaid the £2.5 million refurbishment costs. If The Queen was distressed by the couple's decision to leave the UK she managed to conceal it with her usual skill, saying that Harry and Meghan would always remain much loved members of the family.

Then, on 9 April 2021, came the news that was truly the saddest personal blow for The Queen. Buckingham Palace issued the following announcement:

'It is with deep sorrow that Her Majesty The Queen announces the death of her beloved husband, His Royal Highness The Prince Philip, Duke of Edinburgh. His Royal Highness passed away peacefully this morning at Windsor Castle. The Royal Family join with people around the world in mourning his loss.'

On 9 March 2020, the Duke and Duchess of Sussex made their last public appearance as working members of the Royal Family when they joined The Queen and other senior members of the Royal Family at the Commonwealth Day service at Westminster Abbey.

On 2 August 2017, the Duke of Edinburgh attended a parade in his role as Captain General of the Royal Marines, his last solo public engagement following the announcement in May that he was to retire from public duty.

Prince Philip was 99 years old, just two months short of his 100th birthday. When he was 96, he retired from official royal duties, with 'the full support of The Queen' who had been urging him to take things a little easier. Since his wife came to the throne in 1952, Prince Philip had travelled to dozens of countries and made over 600 solo overseas visits, in addition to those when he accompanied The Queen. Altogether, he carried out 22,219 solo engagements and gave 5,496 speeches as part of his patronage of 785 organisations, both civilian and military.

He had been showered with honours by his wife. In 1957, ten years after they were married, she created him a Prince of the United Kingdom, a title her father, King George VI, had denied his son-in-law. And as a birthday present when he reached 90 in 2011, The Queen made her husband Lord High Admiral, while in November 2017, on the 70th anniversary of their wedding, The Queen appointed Philip to be a Knight Grand Cross of the Royal Victorian Order, her personal Order of Chivalry, for his services to the sovereign.

The Royal Household swung into action with its usual precision as soon as the announcement of Prince Philip's death was made, activating Operation Forth Bridge, the code name for his funeral. The service took place on 17 April starting at 2.40pm. It was a Ceremonial Royal Funeral rather than a State Funeral, the latter usually reserved only for the monarch. Prince Philip had made all the arrangements himself many years before, but there were certain restrictions owing to the Covid-19 pandemic, which included the congregation at the funeral service having to wear masks. The Duke's coffin was taken to St George's Chapel in Windsor on a Land Rover he had designed himself, and the service, which was broadcast live on television and radio, was a family occasion with unique personal touches as previously requested by Philip. The congregation, if in uniform, wore day dress with medals, otherwise mourning clothes. The younger members of the Royal Family walked behind the coffin while The Queen rode in the State Bentley. The funeral service lasted for just 50 minutes and was conducted by the Dean of Windsor, David Conner, with the Archbishop of Canterbury, Justin Welby, giving the blessing. At the conclusion of the very moving service, a Royal Marine bugler played the 'Last Post' followed by 'Action Stations', again at Prince Philip's request.

For The Queen it was a fitting and poignant finale for the man to whom she had been married for 73 years.

The Duke of Edinburgh's coffin is carried into St George's Chapel for his funeral service.

The ultimate professional: on 11 May 2021, just a month after the death of the Duke of Edinburgh, Her Majesty Queen Elizabeth II walks behind the Imperial State Crown, carried on a cushion, as she processes to her seat for the State Opening of Parliament.

THE 2010S

The new millennium had already seen the introduction of the iPod and Facebook, the death of Pope John Paul II, and Barack Obama elected as the first black President of the United States. The year 2012 saw celebrations to mark Her Majesty's Diamond Jubilee; that same year the Olympic Games were held in London (with The Queen joining in the fun by seemingly jumping out of a helicopter with 007 James Bond). In 2016, the UK voted to leave the European Union. In June 2021, in line with Covid-19 restrictions, a reduced Trooping the Colour Parade was held at Windsor Castle.

And the decade ended on a high note when 18-year-old schoolgirl Emma Raducanu became the first female British tennis player in 44 years to win a Grand Slam when she won the US Open in New York, receiving a personal message of congratulations from Her Majesty.

LEFT: The boy who will be King: Prince Charles at Balmoral with his parents and sister in 1953, in the early days of Queen Elizabeth II combining the roles of monarch, wife and mother.

OPPOSITE: The Queen looks to the sky as the Red Arrows perform the fly-past at her official Birthday Parade, held at Windsor Castle in 2021.

The Future

The office of a Queen Regnant is arguably the loneliest in the world, especially if she has been recently widowed, without anyone of equal rank to turn to for advice and reassurance. And when one has acceded to the throne at the tender age of 25, having been married for only five years, the difficulties must at first have seemed more than a little intimidating. The shock of being propelled from the comparative obscurity of life as a young wife and mother (albeit also being a royal Princess) with her husband, a serving officer, anticipating a brilliant career in the Royal Navy, to becoming, at a stroke, the most famous woman on earth, would have made anyone a little apprehensive, to say the least. But if it did, Her Majesty gave no outward sign of it.

In those early days, Queen Elizabeth II managed to cope magnificently with the extraordinary pressures of combining the roles of wife, mother and sovereign. Now she combines her roles just as efficiently with that of widow, a tribute to her

The Queen, the Prince of Wales, the Duchess of Cornwall and the Duke and Duchess of Cambridge at the Eden Project in Cornwall in June 2021, where leaders from the United Kingdom, the USA, Canada, France, Germany, Italy and Japan met for the G7 (Group of 7) summit.

single-minded devotion to duty, along with her love and affection for her country and her family.

Her Majesty has outlasted Prime Ministers, Presidents, Popes and every other Head of State, during her 70 years on the British throne. She has enjoyed an unrivalled position from which to view the rest of the world and she is the perfect example of what a constitutional monarch should be, working tirelessly as an executive professional for the House of Windsor. Despite being well into her 90s, Her Majesty generally enjoys excellent health, although in autumn 2021 she spent a night in King Edward VII's Hospital in London (known locally as Sister Agnes's) for investigation, and was encouraged by her doctors to cancel her official engagements for two weeks and only undertake light desk-based duties. However, during this period she even made reference to her own mortality – 'none of us will live forever' – when she spoke on 1 November via video link to world leaders at the COP26 global climate summit in Glasgow about the need for action to create a safer future for our planet 'for our children and our children's children, and those who will follow in their footsteps'.

The Queen's Baton Relay is held around the world in the lead up to the Commonwealth Games, which take place every four years. Here at Buckingham Palace on 7 October 2021, The Queen passes the baton to British parasport athlete Kadeena Cox at the launch of the relay for the XXII Commonwealth Games, taking place in Birmingham in 2022.

During the latter part of the 20th century and in the early years of the 21st, Buckingham Palace, that symbol of power and authority, experienced a certain amount of criticism, mainly due to the behaviour of some of the younger members of the Royal Family, yet none of the attacks was directed at The Queen herself, apart from that single occasion following the death of Diana, Princess of Wales. Her Majesty's demeanour has always been of the highest quality and if she felt any anger at the public's disapproval, no one outside her own family ever knew of it. Indeed, courtiers said the only emotion they could sense was a slight confusion on her part.

Her Majesty has always been a traditionalist and firm believer in maintaining the practices and protocol of the monarchy, yet she has never opposed any of the ideas of modernisation as proposed by the Prince of Wales and the late Duke of Edinburgh, even though one or two may have privately appalled her. The Queen is also a realist who has been prepared to adapt to changing circumstances and who

The Queen with her eldest children, Charles and Anne, at the annual Braemar Royal Highland Gathering in 2018.

LEFT: Two future kings: Prince Charles and Prince William with their wives, the Duchess of Cornwall and the Duchess of Cambridge, at the Royal Albert Hall in London in September 2021.

OPPOSITE: The Queen and her three heirs watch the fly-past at Trooping the Colour 2019. To Her Majesty's right stands the heir apparent, her eldest son, Prince Charles; on the left of the group are her grandson Prince William and great-grandson Prince George (second and third in line to the throne).

embraced multiculturalism in Britain long before it became an accepted part of the country's consciousness.

Although now in his eighth decade, Prince Charles will one day become the immediate future, followed, of course, by William and Catherine. The structure of the Royal Family will change, particularly with the self-imposed exile of Harry and Meghan. Prince Charles has already indicated that he would prefer a more slimmed-down working Royal Family, with only the immediate family of himself, Camilla, William, Catherine and Anne, The Princess Royal, plus Edward and Sophie undertaking public duties. A hopeful omen for the future is that Prince Charles is so willing to accept change; his concern for the environment, among his many causes, and the totality of his enthusiasms, are also encouraging and reassuring. In addition, William and Catherine's demonstrated care for the under-privileged is well known, hopeful and optimistic.

William will become Prince of Wales when his father accedes to the throne but he has already stressed that he does not want the pomp and ceremony of a full ceremonial investiture as Charles endured at Caernarfon Castle in 1969.

LEFT: The Duchess of Cambridge with two kings-in-waiting: her husband, Prince William, and their eldest son, Prince George. The family celebrates as England scores a goal at the UEFA European Football Championship at Wembley Stadium in London, June 2021.

The Queen's role as Head of the Commonwealth is as important to her as that of being Queen of the United Kingdom. As Kenneth Kaunda (President of Zambia 1964–91), who was one of her earliest friends in the organisation when she first became its leader, once said, 'She is the cement that holds us all together.' If the Commonwealth has survived and prospered through many turbulent years, it is mainly because of her influence and that must be regarded as an integral part of her achievements.

For many people, though, the real and lasting success of Queen Elizabeth II is the way in which her position as the focus of British national identity unifies the nation. She is the person to whom the people turn in times of crisis, mourning and celebration. She exemplifies continuity in a rapidly changing world, one in which internationalism has become increasingly accepted. The Queen is widely acknowledged to be responsible for the stability of the monarchy for the past 70 years; her heirs will occupy a throne that has survived and prospered because of her dedication to duty. And, as her successors will find out, in the words of American President Ronald Reagan, 'She will be a hard act to follow.'

Finally, as Queen Elizabeth II celebrates her Platinum Jubilee, we respectfully offer not only our congratulations but also our grateful thanks for Her Majesty's resolute devotion to our interests for 70 years.

Thank you Ma'am.

LEFT: 'Plant a Tree for the Jubilee' is the message of The Queen's Green Canopy (QGC) initiative, encouraging people throughout the UK to do just that to mark Her Majesty's Platinum Jubilee in 2022. Here, on 1 October 2021, The Queen and Prince Charles marked the start of the tree-planting season when they planted a copper beech together at Balmoral.

OPPOSITE: The Queen attended the ceremonial opening of the sixth Senedd – the Welsh Parliament – at Cardiff on 14 October 2021.

ACKNOWLEDGEMENTS

Text by Brian Hoey; the author has asserted his moral rights.

Edited by Gill Knappett
Proofread by Clare Sayer
Picture research by Gill Knappett
Designed by Geoff Borin

Text copyright © Pitkin Publishing 2022.

All photographs used by kind permission of PA Images except for the following, usedby kind permission of Alamy: pp14, 21 (right), 30, 35 (left), 40, 41, 46, 49 (left), 69, 76, 85, 93 (bottom).

A CIP catalogue for this book is available from the British Library.

Pitkin Publishing is an imprint of B.T. Batsford Holdings Ltd
43 Great Ormond Street, London WC1N 3HZ, UK

www.batsford.com
+44 (0)20 7462 1500

Printed in Bell & Bain Limited, UK

ISBN 978-1-84165-939-8   1/22

BRIAN HOEY

Author and broadcaster Brian Hoey has written more than 30 books about royalty and interviewed several members of the Royal Family, including Prince Charles, the Princess Royal, the Duke of Edinburgh and Diana, Princess of Wales. His other royal titles for Pitkin Publishing are:
Queen Elizabeth; Her Majesty, Queen Elizabeth II (Golden Jubilee); Her Majesty Queen Elizabeth II (Diamond Jubilee); Diana, Princess of Wales; Charles and Diana; The Queen and Her Family; Buckingham Palace.

FRONT COVER: The Queen in February 2020, on a visit to MI5's headquarters in London.

PAGE 1: On her 1953–54 Commonwealth tour, The Queen captures the moment with her cine camera

PAGE 2: Princess Elizabeth arrives at a London theatre for a film premiere in 1951.

PAGES 4–5: The Queen in 2012, during a visit to Exeter University as part of her Diamond Jubilee tour of the UK.